Heaven is for Real...
SOMEBODY TOLD ME!

Nemra Rhoden

Power Junction
Springfield MO

Heaven is for Real... Somebody Told Me

Scripture references are taken from the New King James version of the Bible unless otherwise noted.

Published by:
Power Junction
P.O. Box 7097
Springfield, MO 65801
powerjunction@gmail.com
www.powerjunction.org

Cover art and folio by David Knox | DNK Multimedia

ISBN-10: **0578146320**
ISBN-13: **978-0-578-14632-4**

DEDICATION

This book is dedicated to all people who truly seek God's truth. When you find it, then you will have peace, be in health and prosper.

CONTENTS

INTRODUCTION

Gold or fools' gold? A lake in the desert or a perfect mirage? An angel from God or a familiar spirit? A shooting star or fireworks?

"Heaven is For Real" is a feel good movie that is well acted, directed and written. It is based on the visions of a little boy during a near death experience. Christians are divided on whether this film is a wonderful, harmless Christian experience or a disturbing movie as far as biblical values are considered.

The reason why almost everyone accepted that the little boy really was in heaven, including all his experiences, was based on his encounter with "Pop," his great grandfather that he had never met on earth. He also claimed to have met his sister that he never knew about on earth. His sister had died in her mother's tummy at a few months old and the family never had told Colton about it. So how could this boy have known all these things without actually being in heaven and talking directly to them? Is there enough factual proof to make the story real? Is there any danger in believing all that the boy related, especially pointing out a picture of what Jesus looked like? I haven't heard anyone asking questions about this and I have seen many people accept the boy's visions as being something good because of his age alone. The Bible says to test the spirits and that is what this book is about.

I believe this little boy is honest in what he saw, but we must question the source of these visions. You need to make your own decisions about this, whether good or bad, but only after considering all the Biblical facts.

The intent of this book is not to decide if all that happened to the little boy in "Heaven is for Real" is true, or to judge you for what you think concerning this. Rather, I want people to be aware that there are several other possibilities or situations that can explain how Colton could have known the information he received. In other words, there are other sources that can tell us information under the guise of beautiful visions, and it may not be from where or from whom you think.

These are the questions we as Christians should be asking ourselves about this movie:

- Is God the only source of revealing visions?
- Can a small child make a mistake?
- Can a small child be deceived?
- Can Satan use a small child to deceive us?
- Can some other source take on the image of what we think Jesus looks like?
- Can Christians be deceived?
- Would we recognize fallen angels, demons, spirit guides or angels of light if we saw them?
- What are the scriptures to warn God's people of deception?
- Is all beautiful art from God?

- Are "RECEIVERS" to the spiritual world good or bad?
- Can appearances of relatives who have gone on before us be explained?
- What does "test the spirits" in the Bible mean?
- Is the scripture *"Even the very elect if they could be deceived"* a warning that all that glitters is not gold?

Matthew 24:24 *"For false christs and false prophets will arise and show great signs and wonders to deceive, if possible, even the very elect."*

CONSIDER THIS

People can, with the purest of intentions, promote all kinds of things and not necessarily recognize the entire agenda behind them.

According to Webster's Dictionary, deception means the act of deceiving someone: "an act or statement intended to make people believe something that is not true." We could be tricked or deceived by emotions, our senses, peers, lies, camouflage, false knowledge, and most importantly, lack of knowledge. So how do we know when we are being deceived? The first source a Christian should use to consider what is truth is the Bible, the only true document proven to have withstood the test of time. Direction from the Holy Spirit is important, as well as developing discernment. If we renew our minds daily as the scripture says, then we can assimilate knowledge from the Bible more accurately.

Romans 12:2 *"And do not be conformed to this world, but be transformed by the renewing of your mind, that you may prove what is that good and acceptable and perfect will of God."*

Words or phrases that must be studied to help recognize if there is deception around us are:

- angel of light
- wolves in sheep's clothing
- "even the very could be deceived if possible"
- Father of Lies
- deception
- false doctrine
- "If an angel ...preaches any other gospel..."

There are two types of people in the world. One type would say what they see and what they hear is enough proof to believe something. The other type would say "sure, I heard that but what are the facts around the statement," or "sure, I saw it, but did I really see all that was there?" I am not making any judgment whether one type of person is better than another, only that there are those who research and those who do not.

A comparison for this point is to consider two groups of people on a camping trip. The first group comes upon a cave. As they look at the cave's opening they might say, "that's really cool, sure looks dark in there. Probably bats and spiders inside. Let's not go in and just keep on the hiking trail." As the second group sees the opening of the cave they may say, "a cave! Who has a flashlight? Let's check it out and maybe we can discover what might be in there."

If the first group describes you, you may not want to read any further. On the other hand, if the second group describes you then you are going to go on a intriguing journey through truth.

CAUTION! READ ON AT YOUR OWN RISK!

RULE # 1
TO DISCOVER TRUTH

Never base your beliefs on what seems to be the innocence of a child!

A charming, innocent child could have really seen or heard something so it may seem believable in what they say. But at a young age, children are not capable of knowing exactly where the true source of information may have come from.

An example of this is when I went to an illusionist show recently. All the little kids were excited when at the very end of the show, a huge airplane appeared on stage in a matter of seconds. The children believed it was a real plane; after all, they saw it with their own eyes. The matured adults who knew about air compressors and blow up balloons (like the kind used in Macy's Thanksgiving parade) knew it was not real.

We all want to believe what a small child says but our heart should not overtake reality or factual truth. When we research and renew our hearts and minds through God's word, only then can we accurately discover the agenda behind things, whether it is to lift up the gospel or to trap people into subtle lies leading to false doctrine.

In the movie "Heaven is for Real," a 3 year old boy claims he saw Jesus. It certainly is possible but Christians need to ask the question: "Can demons take on the form of loved ones and deceive us?" Could something other than the true Jesus appear to any one and be a spirit in disguise? The Bible clearly states to **TEST THE SPIRITS!**

The boy's beliefs may have been innocent, but what was behind the spirits that appeared to him? Was it really his sister and great grandpa, or could it have been angels, familiar spirits or spirit guides? Would you know the difference? Would a child know the difference? Maybe this boy really saw Jesus, but my concern is that many Christians blindly accepted this statement because it came out of the mouth of innocence. Is there a possibility it wasn't Jesus? My point is that we need to question things like this. If it's true then great. If it's a deception then for what reason?

Jesus mentioned wolves in sheep's clothing. Sheep are cuddly, cute, innocent looking and loveable. If the wolf looks and acts like a lamb then we could be fooled. If we don't see any wolves around us then we are in trouble because they are there. You can call it temptation, peers who want to get us into trouble, or even TV shows we really enjoy that promote forms of evil. Maybe there are voices in our head with a message that is totally against God's plan for truth and peace in our lives.

If a child gives a message and starts talking about spiritual visions and everyone attaches themselves to it without question because it made them feel good, then that could lead to trouble. You may say a 3 year old cannot say anything wrong. At what age does it become a possibility for a child to know when they are being deceived?

Although I do not promote psychics, I will be using quotes from Sylvia Browne, who is considered to be one of America's most famous psychics. She wrote several best sellers and appeared on the Montel William's show many times. She proclaimed not only to be a psychic, but also a medium connecting the "Other World" to this world. I am using Sylvia's own words to point out that innocent children at an early age can be vulnerable to visitations by familiar spirits, which are actually evil spirits.

To a Bible believer, Deuteronomy 18:10-11 covers the things we are to avoid, including mediums and those with a Spirit of Divination (psychics). Our all-knowing God knows what trouble these situations could lead us into if we have any kind of fellowship with them.

Concerning age of innocence, from Sylvia's book "The Other Side and Back," she says, "I was 5 when I finally became curious enough to speak up about these 'Other people' that no one else but me seemed to notice." On page 4 Sylvia says, "The most significant event of my childhood... happened when I was eight.... I was naturally playing with a flashlight. Suddenly the light began to grow until my whole bedroom was glowing. From the middle of the glow stepped a tall, serene-looking, smiling dark-haired woman who quietly said, "I come from God, Sylvia. Don't be afraid." Later, Sylvia's grandmother told her "that's your spirit guide. She's here to help you."

Obviously if you refer to the Word of God, these spirit guides were not God's angels but rather part of the deception to involve Sylvia in demonic communications at a young age. This was so that when she was older, she could (and did) influence thousands into the same lies of following the wrong voice. Paranormal things can happen at any age. Children are not the only ones to have visions or encounters with good or evil angels. Again, I must say, I believe the boy in "Heaven is for Real" actually saw things. Once more, the question we need to ask is, "could these visions have been from a different source other then God?"

Any Angel of Light can use words like Love, Hope, Peace, God, Jesus and use them freely. Remember, Satan himself tried to tempt the real Jesus in the wilderness by using scripture. As a matter of fact, the New Age movement uses these words. They almost turn the concept of love into a god.

Satan Tempts Jesus

Matthew 4:1-11 *"Then Jesus was led up by the Spirit into the wilderness to be tempted by the devil. And when He had fasted forty days and forty nights, afterward He was hungry. Now when the tempter came to Him, he said, "If You are the Son of God, command that these stones become bread." But He answered and said, "It is written, 'Man shall not live by bread alone, but by every word that proceeds from the mouth of God.'" Then the devil took Him up into the holy city, set Him on the pinnacle of the temple, and said to Him, "If You are the Son of God, throw Yourself down. For it is written 'He shall give His angels charge over you, 'and,' In their hands they shall bear you up, ,Lest you dash your foot against a stone.'" Jesus said to him, "It is written again, 'You shall not tempt the LORD your God. '"Again, the devil took Him up on an exceedingly high mountain, and showed Him all the kingdoms of the world and their glory. And he said to Him, "All these things I will give You if You will fall down and worship me." Then Jesus said to him, "Away with you, Satan! For it is written, 'You shall worship the LORD your God, and Him only you shall serve. '"Then the devil left Him, and behold, angels came and ministered to Him."*

TEST THE SPIRITS

Spirit Guides, Familiar Spirits, Fallen Angels

1 John 4:1 *"Beloved, do not believe every spirit, but test the spirits, whether they are of God: because many false prophets have gone out into the world."*

What is a Spirit Guide?

The next two paragraphs are an excerpt from my book "CANDY COATED OCCULT" page 138:

'A "Spirit Guide" is a guide or voice from another realm or time that directs you, or shares knowledge with you. The spirit may take form, talk audibly, talk to your mind or talk through automatic handwriting. These spirits are not of God so they promote reincarnation as a truth. Spirit guides are demons wearing a coat of wisdom that hides their sinister intentions.

I would like to note here that in 2003, Sylvia Browne...was promoting her book on how to contact your spirit guides. She said, "you need to know your spirit guide, your angels, your Christ-consciousness, your holy spirit." She is proof of the occult being 'gray,' because she combined the Holy Spirit with spirit guides. To God, this division is black and white. The new millennium is awaking people's access to demons.'

What could be the reasons for the innocent little boy to have seen all the things he did (the stories about dead relatives and the descriptions of things at age three that he couldn't have otherwise known)? Ask yourself, "can children be deceived?"

The big question is, how could Colton have known about 'Pop' or his little sister? Surely this is proof he went to Heaven and all of his encounters were real.

Hey, not so fast! As Christians we should do what the word of God says which is to TEST THE SPIRITS. One way to do this is to ask the question, "could Colton have gotten his information from any other source?" The answer is YES. Colton obviously was involved in a near- death experience and really saw something. What we must ask is, "was it a beautiful show put on by spirit guides to seduce people into believing a possible lie or was it a genuine experience presented by God?"

Spirit guides, also known as angels of light or fallen angels, can walk, talk, and take on various appearances. They have a networking system of communication like none other. A spirit can gleen knowledge from any place in time and share with other spirits. The receivers, which I will talk about later, can hear from these spirits and then know any information from the past or present. A child or person of any age can obtain this information without necessarily asking for it. So Colton could have heard these things about his family from disguised deceivers of the spirit world.

An example of demonic networking is taken from my book, "The Truth About Psychics" page 10.

'One particular time my friends and I were playing with a Ouija Board. As I placed my hands on the plastic pointer, it quickly started to move back and forth. It swiftly spelled out the message "Mr. Strong is dead." Just then our telephone rang and my mother answered the phone. She was told that Mr. Strong had died a couple of hours earlier. He had fallen through the ice at a lake, about seventy miles away. Mr. Strong was a friend of the family so we were notified not long after his death. How did the Ouija Board receive the information? A demon (spirit) witnessed Mr. Strong's death and informed the spirit running our game board. I suppose this situation was supposed to make us trust the powers of the Ouija Board, but instead it just "frightened us."'

It is vital to understand that Spirits can relay information to even innocent children and the knowledge received be accurate as well as be deceitful. There are good angels all throughout the Bible for protection, warnings, praise, ministering to the saints and so on, but beware of the evil ones disguised as light!

If we do not know the difference between God's angels and Satan's angels, then we could be following the whims of demons disguised as beautiful beings. We could actually be giving demons an audience and not even recognize it.

2 Corinthians 11:14 *"And no wonder! For Satan himself transforms himself into an angel of light."*

Luke 18:16 *"But Jesus called them to Him, and said, "let the little children come to Me, and do not forbid them : for of such is the kingdom of God."*

While interviewing Colton, news reporters have quoted the above scripture as proof that everything he experienced is from Jesus, therefore all his accounts must be acceptable. This scripture relates that Jesus wants children to come to Him, just as He wants all of us to come to Him, but not all of us heed the call. "Such as the kingdom of Heaven" would include the innocence of a child accepting Jesus for who He is and loving God with a pure heart. But nowhere does the scripture state that 100% of all children are perfect. As a matter of record the Word of God states that we are all born with a sin nature. The Bible also mentions that we should train up a child in the way he should go. Without truth and right direction, a child can be misled into destructive paths of life. A child needs direction in order to learn truth.

Once as a young child, during my sleep I had a dream, or vision, of meeting and being in the presence of a new friend, someone who seemed to care for me. She was in physical form. I could see and hear her perfectly. What I remember most is the wonderful, peaceful feeling as she spoke. I was talking to this special someone in a different plane. It wasn't on earth. During this short visit with her, I felt love and I felt this girl would now be my best friend. She said her name was Jessie. I wanted her to give me something to hold on to so I could remember our meeting but she said nothing material could cross over. Right then I tried to hold her hand. I didn't want to leave her company, but I quickly woke up with nothing in my hand. I was left with a sadness because my new friend from the other side was somewhere else and I may never see her again.

This story is to let you know that very young children can have spirit encounters with evil or good. In my case I wouldn't realize until I was older and received Jesus Christ as my Savior, that Jessie was not from God and had evil intentions. I also learned that you can have peace in the presence of evil. I now recognize that Jessie was a familiar spirit awakening me to the spirit of divination by believing in spirit communication. She set a trap and I fell in. Thank God I was delivered from all forms of divination and now I only trust the Word of God and the Holy Spirit.

Children have reported having spiritual encounters even when they are very little. Because I came out of an occult type background, I can testify to these visions. More importantly, children have confided in me of unexplainable things they have seen.

One little boy told his mother he saw angels around him while playing outside. He was about 4.

Maybe they were God's protective angels, but maybe they were familiar spirits or spirit guides. I believe the children actually can see something. but they are not necessarily capable of discerning good from evil.

The world holds to the belief of "Spirit Guides" as good as promoted by Sylvia Browne as well as Oprah. Here are a few of God's warnings about spirit guides.

1 Timothy 4:1 *"Now the Spirit expressly says that in later times some will depart from the faith, giving heed to deceiving spirits and doctrines of demons..."*

2 Corinthians 11:14-15 *"And no wonder! For Satan himself transforms himself into an angel of light. Therefore it is no great thing if his ministers also transform themselves into ministers of righteousness, "whose end will be according to their works..."*

In the trailer of "Heaven is for Real," did you know there are 3 images that would fit the description of a spirit guide. They are hard to notice at first but once you know they are there, they are clearly seen. One is a fast moving man in the hallway of the Burpo house. At the end of the movie trailer a lady in church sees the image of her son that had died. The third I found by accident. It is an image strongly resembling "Pop". He is standing in the shadows amongst a crowd of people. Why were they put in the trailer? For what purpose?

While I was in college, I began to clearly see spirits in the form of people who had passed on.

Usually they were standing behind a person that I was reading palms for. (I did not read the Bible at this time in my life and I was under the illusion that psychic intuition was a gift. I'm glad I'm delivered from all those lies! No more palm reading, no more talking to spirits.) Anyway, when I would describe the person I was seeing, my friends would say, "that's my grandma," or "that's my uncle who died a while ago." So I know for a fact that if a person is open to the spirit world at any age, you can have visits from spirits or familiar spirits. Now I know that once a person dies there is a great divide between them and us. They can no longer come to us. As in the story in the Bible of the rich man and the poor beggar, they cannot cross over. Know that a familiar spirit can take on the form of someone that has died, a loved one, or of anyone they want. Beware of angels of light! Ask God for discernment on these things to be able to know the difference.

A familiar spirit can refer to a "fallen angel" that takes on the form of a deceased person familiar to you. We get a false sense of comfort in seeing an apparition of a relative that died, but is that really your relative?

These deceptive angels have been around thousands and thousands of years. A familiar spirit may also be a spirit that has traveled in your family for decades, promoting alcoholism, lust, divination or other evil intentions. Appearances of people that have gone before us should send up a red flag.

The Holy Spirit should be our comfort, not ghosts, spirit guides or familiar spirits. There is also comfort in knowing that Jesus came to mend the broken-hearted.

Psalm 147:2-3 *"The LORD builds up Jerusalem; He gathers together the outcasts of Israel. He heals the brokenhearted And binds up their wounds."*

Because of my past of having visions similar to Colton in respect to relatives that have gone on, I discovered certain people are "RECEIVERS." I choose this word because that is what some people starting at a very young age can do. That is to receive messages, visions, and different forms of communication from outside this earthly plane. I believe some people are born with a gift of being more sensitive to the spiritual world than others. If a "receiver" has not sold out to God by making Jesus Christ their Lord and Savior and repenting of their sins, then it is easy to be drawn into the illusions presented to us. Signs and all wonders can also include visions of so called people in heaven, but those people not necessarily being who they say they are. The object here is to recognize there are good visions and there are false visions. Do not assume all visions, even by children, are good.

The Word of God is clear that Satan is powerful with signs and all wonders of evil which can include visions. The devil is a masterful deceiver and uses light and forms of it. The Bible also warns us that angels can be evil yet disguised as beautiful. Beware Christians! All that glitters is not gold. Fool's gold deceived many. A mirage in the desert has deceived many. A snare is set to win and take hearts away from God's truth.

KNOW THE ENEMY HAS A DECISIVE PLAN TO DECEIVE YOU OVER TIME

1 Peter 5:8 *"Be sober, be vigilant; because your adversary the devil walks about like a roaring lion, seeking whom he may devour.*

John 10:10 *"The thief does not come except to steal, and to kill, and to destroy. I have come that they may have life, and that they may have it more abundantly."*

Jeremiah 14:14 And the LORD said to me, *"The prophets prophesy lies in My name. I have not sent them, commanded them, nor spoken to them; they prophesy to you a false vision, divination, a worthless thing, and the deceit of their heart.*

In John chapter 8, Satan is referred to as the *"Father of Lies."* He can try to fool anyone of us if possible in any way he thinks we could believe. The only thing that points us to truth is God's word.

Ask the Question, Does symbolism matter?

Compare our spiritual enemy's tactics to that of a general during a war. By the way, even in our everyday routines the enemy does not take a holiday from trying to convince us of false truths. We may not see all the spiritual activities and spirits around us but they are there. I love the scriptures God has given us for protection and comfort to ward off evil doings around us, but God also expects us to know our adversary.

An example from the movie "Heaven is for Real" is the boy who said he saw Jesus was always holding a Spider-Man toy. It seemed the movie's director made a point that the toy be present in many shots during the movie. This validated Spider-Man to young viewers since this cute little boy was holding it so much. When he dropped his Spider-Man toy going into the operating room, it seemed to be symbolic of the boy's life energy being drained from his body. When the boy recovered from his near death experience, the first thing he said was, "I want to hold the spider" (which would be Rosie the friendly tarantula). If you just had a vision of Jesus and heaven, would a spider be the first thing on your mind? A Spider symbol was probably used to let the audience know he wasn't afraid of anything anymore and everything was going to be alright because he had been with Jesus, but is there more to it?

Consider Spider-Man's symbolic hand gesture. It is identical to the Satanic sign of fellowship with others of the same belief. Research pictures of rock stars, Illuminati, and Satanists, and you will see that hand symbol being proudly displayed. Secondly, spiders in many ancient mythologies represent an occult or pagan power as well as a life force.

"Examples: in Ancient Pre-Mexican Civilization the "Great goddess was the Spider woman." (1)

"In Ancient Egypt, the spider was used as a symbol to represent the goddess of the Divine Mother, Neith. In some American Indian tribes, it is considered as the symbol for the creator of the world and by extension is associated with the female creative energy.

In Native Hopi Cosmology the Creator of the Universe is known as Grandmother Spider. In

Babylonia mythology the goddess Ishtar was often depicted as a Spider and her symbol was an eight-rayed pointed star representing the eight legs of a spider.

The 'third eye' in other religions represents the Pineal Gland in our brain. It is referred to as "our great spider, our higher self or daemon located in the precise center of our brain web. In pagan meditation (by chanting aum) they say we can tap the web in our brain and be enlightened to higher consciousness." (2)

These are New Age themes. So in the movie is the Spider-Man toy and references to the tarantula just a coincidence or subliminal messages for other reasons?

FALSE IMAGES

The First Commandment given to Moses was:

Exodus 20:2-3 *"I am the LORD your God, who brought you out of the land of Egypt, out of the house of bondage. You shall have no other gods before Me."*

For someone to say, *"That is what Jesus looks like,"* is very dangerous.

God doesn't need to explain Himself. For example, when God gave the 10 Commandments and said "Thou shall not steal," you will notice He didn't explain why stealing was wrong or harmful. He could have said because you could go to jail or the people you steal from could be emotionally scarred from losing the items you took. Maybe even the thing you have stolen could cause circumstances leading to the death of yourself or someone else.

The point is when God has given us direction on things in life he knows all the circumstances around it and we don't.

In the first commandment, it is clear: no other gods. Be careful not to accept any statue, painting, photograph, hologram or other images that anyone says is your God.

The picture that Akiane Kramarik painted, "Prince of Peace." was shown at the end of the movie "Heaven is for Real." The little boy said that is what Jesus looks like.

The art work of Akiana is amazing and it's beauty cannot be denied. However, if you listen to an interview with Akiana (KCTS 9 in 2010) in relation to her family's walk with God she says, "We went through almost everything from Christian to Catholic to Buddhism. My siblings have their own path, their own spiritual enlightenment that they are reaching. I have my own, my parents have theirs. I cannot say what they believe in or what path they are choosing... for me I am the same person that I was at 4. Since nobody taught me who God was, I found God myself. I don't belong to any denomination or any religion. I just belong to God. I'm spiritual." Her quotes have a new age flair to them. These thoughts could compliment a one-world religion.

I always wondered why the people who walked with Jesus and penned the New Testament never mentioned the psychical features of Jesus. They write all about his teachings and what He stood for but not how tall or short he was, whether his eyes were blue, brown, black or green, or if he had dark or light skin. Why is it that these things are not mentioned? The answer is simple. This is where faith comes in.

First of all, if God wanted us to know the psychical attributes of Jesus it would be stated in the Bible. Consider that the very men who walked with Jesus, who were inspired by the Holy Spirit, did not describe the features of Jesus. God knew that could cause separation and other ethnic rivalries. We know Jesus was a Nazarene, but his features could have been soft or harsh, dark or light. Many paintings try to capture the essence of what Jesus may look like, but a red flag should go up when a little boy or anyone else says "that is what Jesus looks like." (Note that in Revelation when John described Jesus he did not paint a picture for us to see but rather a written account. It was also for prophecy.)

A couple thousand years ago a beautiful young girl in Egypt had an amazing gift of design and sculpture. One day an angel appeared to her and commissioned a golden statue to be designed. The young girl, always anxious to use her gifts, proceeded to work on this statue with beauty and grace until it was finally completed. This lovely work of art only stood about three feet tall but was a wonder to look at. The village's people said, "This is so amazing! It is like our god and it surely was inspired by an angel." That belief spread throughout the land and now the people had an image of what they thought their god looked like. It was made of beautiful gold layered with silver around its eyes and had two horns crowned with rubies on the top of it's head.

This story is fiction of course, but compare this to works of art people may create in the world today. Should we be quick to say "this is so amazing it is like our god" based on it's beauty alone or because a child said "surely this is what our god looks like?" We need to become aware of the Bible's truth and not decide anything solely based on any feelings we receive from any experience.

Without faith we cannot please God. It wouldn't take much faith to believe in God if I had a picture of Him in the flesh. God wants us to know Him by His fruits. That is how he wants us to know the truth of anyone "by their fruits." God is discovered in His creation which is all around us. He is discovered in His works when He was on Earth, even through His Word in the Bible. We please God by knowing He exists without His picture. If we see a picture of what anyone claims to be Jesus, even if a child said it, then we might seek after the person with that face if he were to appear one day.

Here is a thought for you. What if the anti-Christ resembles the picture painted by Akiana? Did you consider this could be possible? After all, Satan was known for his beauty and light as well as trickery and deceit!

Did you know that some artists and poets can be involved with automatic handwriting without even knowing it? Not all gifted people have gotten entangled with this, but it is a form of psychic energy and it does exist.

WHAT IS AUTOMATIC HANDWRITING? Before I turned my life over to Jesus Christ I could place a pen on paper and then watch beautiful words of reflection flow gracefully across the page. Poetry and thought- provoking phrases seemed to pour out of my spirit. I had no idea at the time I was receiving these things from my "spirit guides." In other words, it was demonic influenced. It was wrong to give my mind over to whoever or whatever in the universe that wanted to speak to me. Another situation of peace in the presence of evil. Because I didn't read the Bible, I didn't realize that I was involved with the wrong spirits. From my experience, I know that all art or words are not always from God. It is true, wonderful things do come from God, but not everything.

Beautiful art can be a gift to mankind but not all of it. We can learn to listen to God's voice but we must first be aware that there are other voices calling to us. Can you separate the voices that call you? God does speak to us through the Holy Spirit. Jesus himself said in John 10:27 *"My sheep hear My voice, and I know them, and they follow Me."*

WHAT DID HE SAY?

Colton, the little boy who had the vision, was being interviewed on TV. He said he saw God the Father, sat next to the Holy Spirit for a while, and also sat on the lap of Jesus.

Let us consider if this is possible.

Throughout the Bible many people have seen Jesus in visions and in the flesh.

About seeing the Holy Spirit...

Although there are scriptures about Him, there are no scriptures to prove or disprove what the Holy Spirit really looks like. The description at the baptism of Jesus by John the Baptist doesn't say He was a dove , it says He came down as a dove.

John 1:32-33 *"And John bore witness, saying, "I saw the Spirit descending from heaven like a dove, and He remained upon Him. I did not know Him, but He who sent me to baptize with water said to me, 'Upon whom you see the Spirit descending, and remaining on Him, this is He who baptizes with the Holy Spirit.'*

About seeing God the Father......

1st John 4:12 *"No one has seen God at any time."*

1 Tim. 6:15-16 (Amplified Version) *Which [appearing] will be shown forth in His own proper time by the blessed, only Sovereign (Ruler), the King of kings and the Lord of lords, Who alone has immortality [in the sense of exemption from every kind of death] and lives in unapproachable light, Whom no man has ever seen or can see. Unto Him be honor and everlasting power and dominion. Amen (so be it)."*

Matthew 24:3-5 *"Now as He sat on the Mount of Olives, the disciples came to Him privately, saying, "Tell us, when will these things be? And what will be the sign of Your coming, and of the end of the age?"* And Jesus answered and said to them: *"Take heed that no one deceives you. For many will come in My name, saying, 'I am the Christ,' and will deceive many."*

Matthew 24:23-26 *"Then if anyone says to you, 'Look, here is the Christ!' or 'There!' do not believe it. For false christs and false prophets will rise and show great signs and wonders to deceive, if possible, even the elect. See, I have told you beforehand. "Therefore if they say to you, 'Look, He is in the desert!' do not go out; or 'Look, He is in the inner rooms!' do not believe it."*

If you listen to live interviews of Colton and his dad, some interesting concepts come to light. Heaven seems to take the place of God for comfort.

Mr. Burpo said, "Well, I didn't have doubts about heaven's existence, but I had a lot of questions about what heaven is like." For a Pastor to come up to you and say they got it all figured out they're just not being honest. The Bible has many verses about it but not a complete picture in there. And so for him (Colton) to fill in the blanks and put those pieces together helped me out tremendously and I think it's helping a lot of other people out the same way." Colton says, "People, they want Heaven. They want to know there's something after life."

Mr. Burpo continues in regards to people's questions: "Is someone going to fix what I am going through right now? Is there hope on the other end? You know the pain and stuff we go through in this world, this is not heaven yet. Is it going to get better and is that a reality? And that's where heaven, and knowing that, changes everything, not only how you do life now." (3)

If you look at this statement you could paraphrase it like this: "I know there is a heaven. There is no pastor that can explain heaven and if he tries, he is a liar. Because my son had a vision, I now know heaven is real. He fills in the scriptures that are left out describing heaven. My son has the answers so now we can all be comforted. Now I know there is life after death."

Consider that the scriptures are already clear that there is life after death. It doesn't take a vision from a 3 year old to confirm this.

HEAVEN

The last question of this book is this: "should our faith about the things in heaven be based on a child's vision or should it come from faith in God's written Word?"

Revelation 21:10-27 *"And he carried me away in the Spirit to a great and high mountain, and showed me the great city, the holy Jerusalem, descending out of heaven from God, having the glory of God. Her light was like a most precious stone, like a jasper stone, clear as crystal. Also she had a great and high wall with twelve gates, and twelve angels at the gates, and names written on them, which are the names of the twelve tribes of the children of Israel: three gates on the east, three gates on the north, three gates on the south, and three gates on the west."*

"Now the wall of the city had twelve foundations, and on them were the names of the twelve apostles of the Lamb. And he who talked with me had a gold reed to measure the city, its gates, and its wall. The

city is laid out as a square; its length is as great as its breadth. And he measured the city with the reed: twelve thousand furlongs. Its length, breadth, and height are equal. Then he measured its wall: one hundred and forty-four cubits, according to the measure of a man, that is, of an angel. The construction of its wall was of jasper; and the city was pure gold, like clear glass. The foundations of the wall of the city were adorned with all kinds of precious stones: the first foundation was jasper, the second sapphire, the third chalcedony, the fourth emerald, the fifth sardonyx, the sixth sardius, the seventh chrysolite, the eighth beryl, the ninth topaz, the tenth chrysoprase, the eleventh jacinth, and the twelfth amethyst. The twelve gates were twelve pearls: each individual gate was of one pearl. And the street of the city was pure gold, like transparent glass."

"But I saw no temple in it, for the Lord God Almighty and the Lamb are its temple. The city had no need of the sun or of the moon to shine in it, for the glory of God illuminated it. The Lamb is its light. And the nations of those who are saved shall walk in its light, and the kings of the earth bring their glory and honor into it. Its gates shall not be shut at all by day (there shall be no night there). And they shall bring the glory and the honor of the nations into it. But there shall by no means enter it anything that defiles, or causes an abomination or a lie, but only those who are written in the Lamb's Book of Life."

Revelation 22:1-5 *"And he showed me a pure river of water of life, clear as crystal, proceeding from the throne of God and of the Lamb. In the middle of its street, and on either side of the river, was the tree of life, which bore twelve fruits, each tree yielding its fruit every month. The leaves of the tree were for the healing of the nations. And there shall be no more curse, but the throne of God and of the Lamb shall be in it, and His servants shall serve Him. They shall see His face, and His name shall be on their foreheads. There shall be no night there: They need no lamp nor light of the sun, for the Lord God gives them light. And they shall reign forever and ever."*

John 14:1-6 *"Let not your heart be troubled; you believe in God, believe also in Me. In My Father's house are many mansions; if it were not so, I would have told you. I go to prepare a place for you. And if I go and prepare a place for you, I will come again and receive you to Myself; that where I am, there you may be also. And where I go you know, and the way you know." Thomas said to Him, "Lord, we do not know where You are going, and how can we know the way?" Jesus said to him, "I am the way, the truth, and the life. No one comes to the Father except through Me."*

Revelation 21:4 *"And God will wipe away every tear from their eyes; there shall be no more death, nor sorrow, nor crying. There shall be no more pain, for the former things have passed away."*
****

ABOUT THE AUTHOR

Nemra Rhoden was raised in a Christian family but discovered what seemed to be psychic abilities at an early age. She mistook that as a gift from God. Nemra could read palms, talk to spirits, see auras, interpret dreams, practice psychometry, and automatic handwriting. Nemra also had a business selling numerology charts. In 1983 while in a night club, over the very loud music Nemra heard a soft, gentle voice say, "Nemra, you are better than this." A few days later Nemra heard that quiet voice again and it said, "Nemra, you cannot serve two Masters." At that very moment everything changed. All the occult toys around her looked evil.

She says, "My heart and mind were totally changed. I saw the evil in the psychic things that were in my life. There was a zeal to seek God's way and never return back to my old way of life. My cry was "Lord, show me your ways. Expose the things in my life that I should get rid of. I want to live for you." I felt God's presence of truth and new beginnings. I was a new creation. Since that time I got out of my Rock n' Roll bands that I had been in for 18 years. I burned all my New Age, Numerology, and Astrology Books. I began to read the Bible for new knowledge. I wanted to seek God's truth, not my own. God directed me to learn to be a clown for Children's ministry and started to teach Children's Church. I began writing Christian and children's songs and have written over 400 of them and recorded 16 albums.. I have written 5 books and have been doing Praise and Worship Music in church for 30 years now. Praise God, He truly set me free!"

It is because I was a practicing psychic and got involved with these things which God has delivered me from, that makes it easy for me to discern some of the spiritual activities our young people may encounter.

Luke 10:19 (King James Version) *"Behold, I give unto you power to tread on serpents and scorpions, and over all the power of the enemy: and nothing shall by any means hurt you."*

Deuteronomy 30:15-16 *"See, I have set before you today life and good, death and evil, in that I command you today to love the LORD your God, to walk in His ways, and to keep His commandments, His statutes, and His judgments, that you may live and multiply; and the LORD your God will bless you in the land which you go to possess."*

FOOTNOTES

Chapter 3 TEST THE SPIRITS

(1)http://www.templeilluminatus.com/group/the-triple-goddess/forum/topics/the-spider-goddess-the-web-she-weaves
(2) www.wikipedia.org

Chapter 5 WHAT DID HE SAY?

(3) Fox News Oct.15, 2012